# Do Plants Eat Sunlight?
# Biology Textbook for Young Learners
## Children's Biology Books

**BABY PROFESSOR**
EDUCATION KIDS

Speedy Publishing LLC
40 E. Main St. #1156
Newark, DE 19711
www.speedypublishing.com
Copyright 2016

Let's Explore the amazing world of plants.

Plants play an important role in our environment.

Humans and animals need plants in order to live. We get our food from plants. Animals also need plants for their specific needs.

There are over two hundred thousand identified species of plants. Two thousand different types of plants are used by humans to make food.

But how do plants live?
What do they need?
How do they make their food?

Read on and learn how plants grow and how they use sunlight to make their food.

Plants take in carbon dioxide and give off oxygen. Humans and animals need oxygen in order to sustain life.

Trees, for example, have amazing roles in our surroundings. They help control air pollution.

They also provide us shade on sunny days. Even on the hottest days of summer, trees and other plants give us cooler temperatures.

Plants are independent. They don't look for their food. They can process their own food. They feed themselves.

Plants have specific needs in order to process their own food. One of the most important plant needs is sunlight.

Without sunlight
plants would die.

Do plants eat
sunlight?
This is what we
will discover.

Why do plants
need light?

Plants need sunlight in order to make their own food through the process known as photosynthesis. Plants get energy from sunlight.

All living things need energy in order to grow. Humans get energy from the food they eat.

# What is
# Photosynthesis?

It is the process used by plants to make their food. In this process, plants get energy from light and turn it to chemical energy.

Through photosynthesis, plants use the sun's energy to turn water from the roots and carbon dioxide from the air to make glucose. It is an energy-rich sugar which plants need.

Photosynthesis literally means to make things with light. Photosynthesis happens in the chloroplasts. These are capsule-like cells in the leaves of plants.

Chloroplasts
contain chlorophyll.
This is the green,
light-capturing
pigment in leaves.

Plants make food through their leaves. Leaves play an important role in the process of photosynthesis. It is where plants make their food. It converts light into a chemical energy.

In the process, oxygen is made. The plants give off the oxygen and humans and animals can use it. As the plants make their food, they take in carbon dioxide from the atmosphere.

The light from
the sun sustains
life on this planet,
including the life
of plants. Plants
grow with light.
Light affects the
growth of plants.

Different kinds of plants need different amount of sunlight in order to grow. Shade plants need moderate amounts of sunlight each day, while full sun plants need more direct sunlight every day.

Some plants will not grow well with too little light. If plants are affected by light shortage their leaves may turn yellow and are too small and their stems are spindly.

Gardeners should know the kind of plants they want to grow in order to give their plants the best chance. They should carefully follow instructions on how to grow certain types of plants.

Although plants are capable of making their own food, some of them need humans to care for them. Gardeners water their plants and expose them to proper sunlight so they can grow very well.

It's not only sunlight that helps plants grow. They also need water, fertile soil, and the right temperature to germinate and grow.

Earth needs plants to sustain its life. Hence, plants are the backbone of all life. Plants support our everyday needs.

Animals are also benefited from plants. For this reason, we should take action to conserve and protect our plants, especially the trees.

Plants help maintain our clean and green environment.

Did you enjoy reading this book? Share this to your friends.